Candles

Poems for adults and short stories
for teens and children

Written by Emily Duchene

London Paola Emerson

Peachy Books Inc.

DEDICATION

This book is gratefully dedicated to the most amazing team of selfless teachers and friends.

To all of our nursing instructors and life coaches: your ability to instruct nurses and teachers in such a diligent and compassionate manner has touched more lives than you will ever know.

To our work-families of nurses, nurse assistants, unit secretaries, housekeepers, phlebotomists, pharmacists and everyone else: Thank you for always putting the best version of yourselves into all that you do. Especially thank you for caring for children with life-threatening illness and children on isolation precautions and being just kind enough that we want to grow up and become nurses. Thank you for being supportive of newly hired employees and for treating every patient as though they were special enough for you to learn a greeting in their language, provide a warm wash cloth before their morning medications and even little things like keeping extra reading glasses and kerchiefs in your locker so that when patients come to the hospital unexpectedly, they have one less thing to worry about.

For everyone that goes the extra mile when no one is watching to display empathy and excellence in all of its forms, this book is dedicated to you. We had you in mind when we wrote the poem, "Invisible People".

To Everyone: thank you for taking steps to take care of our planet. From recycling to community gardens to whatever you do to take care of our lovely planet.

Gratefully yours,

Peachy Books Inc.

Introduction

How do you self-care? Scheduled naps, long baths, at home facials and grooming or even a candle with a book and a cup of coffee. Who doesn't need a bit of an occasional 'time out'?

Candles have long been said to promote relaxation and reduce anxiety. From our books for mature readers to our short stories for younger readers, we have included a "Candle" for new and seasoned readers.

TABLE OF CONTENTS

ABOUT CANDLES

The name of my favorite candle tells me what to expect and allows me to identify it by name. With that in mind, we have written an "About" section before each of our "Candles" as a description of where and what inspired the writing of it. Please enjoy our many takes on life lessons in "Candles".

About a writer's pen

"The pen is mightier than the sword". This famous saying reflects the responsibility that artists do well to consider before conveying a message to the world. We recognize the trust placed in everything that we produce with our "Writer's Pen".

A WRITER'S PEN

A writer's pen can cause mayhem and fuss,

Make a good person cuss

Bring a smile to a child

And still all the while…

A writer's pen can,

Guide a boy to be man,

A girl to be friend

A woman to be wife

Bring joy to a life

Or spread chaos and strife

The power of pen that

God gave to men

To unite or divide

Will start deep within

Oh, the things that will come

From your writer's pen

Alas, you're writing again.

About Homeless

This next poem was inspired by the current situation of so many people around the world. Ordinary, creative, intelligent people that find themselves on the other side of the life that they worked so hard to create.

After years of working in hospitals in the greater Los Angeles area, we have come to know many working professionals, parents and even college graduates that find themselves homeless for one reason or another.

This poem is not about the "free spirits" that actually prefer the anonymity of living off the grid. Yup, met them too. What is the solution?

There are in fact a great deal of organizations that are working to end homelessness in America such as Endhomelessness.org. We have met many hardworking people that work to this end. They work to pair people with their family members, with jobs and even housing assistance and job training. It is our hope that after reading this poem people will be a little more empathetic to both the homed and the homeless.

HOMELESS

I am cold, and in the way

In want

Desperate to fit in

Desiring to get back

Invisible night like black.

To get back…

Back …To normal

Back…To routine

Back…To warm bath

Back…To clean soft sheets

Not by choice

Did I lose my voice?

And place

And face…

I am cold and I'm the way

I was a child of two

Sibling of few, Before life's dent…

Concrete sleeps

Ignoring scents of pee

Hard on back and hips

News-papered benches

Avoiding dog yard fences…

I am cold and in the way

Can't trust a friend

Cause here that'll be my end

If on me they see shine

They'll take what was once mine.

They admire once

And I know it's begun

The plotting to take

My show-off mistake.

Too shiny? Too new?

Gotta break up with this life

Want to wake up from this strife.

A hot meal.

Short spells of quiet.

Basic human kindness.

Warm smile.

Handshakes without gloves.

I am cold and in the way

I once did matter

Before life's core was shattered

My mental became tattered

I'm trying to press reset

But I am too far beset

I was employee of the month

And later had my own

I'm sure they're fully grown.

I am cold and in the way

I had pets and plants

And even a car

A car would be nice

Somewhere dry and safe to sleep

I could move or keep…

Moving.

I had an address

I had neighbors who knew

My daily routine

My self- imposed curfew

I had it all

Or some did say.

Till once came that faithful day

The bottom fell out

There was no turning back

By shock I was blinded and could only see black

The rest is a blur.

I came to

on a curb.

And only could say….

I am cold and, in the way,

Homeless…

Not Hopeless.

About Look at me and see you

Empathy is the inspiration for "Look at me and see you".

We live in a world where people are taught to prejudge.

 Being critical of others is some people's claim to fame. Are they so mean because they're afraid to be kind?

Empathy doesn't have to be a financial hand out.

 It can be an idea like the free WiFi at local libraries,

after school programs, and job training for people in need of assistance.

As nurses, we have cared for people with some of the most tragic circumstances. People whose lives were torn apart by an unexpected illness, or the loss of a loved one.

If you have never found yourself in need of such help that's great.

But if you're in a position to help someone in need, it is our hope that you will choose kindness, choose empathy.

LOOK AT ME AND SEE YOU

Look at me and see you

Look at me and see through

Height, gender, weight or race

Look at me and see your face.

See past my bad choices

Hear me and hear your children's voices.

Look at me and see, not my credit score.

See me

    and

        I'll say this one once more...

See you

ABOUT INVISIBLE PEOPLE

As far back as any recorded history, there have been invisible people. People that have done so much more that they will ever be credited. There are so many mothers, dads, wives, and others whose words or actions have changed history. These unsung persons are the stuff of legend.

There is something to be said for being a "lesser known" fly on the wall. Are there really people that prefer the backstage of life instead of the spotlight?

INVISIBLE PEOPLE

Shade and shadows were made for hot days.

The way that she craves it, would many

amaze.

Her secret power is her anonymity.

She was raised by a mother that could make something out of nothing.

Mom made clothes, food, refinished furniture and of course she had a green

thumb.

She had a PHD in 'lifeology'.,

Strangers can be trusted, because her value they can't see.

So many long for recognition and fame.

That everyone might know their name.

The invisible girl was born like an ant.

Hidden in plain sight with so many at her side.

Talented, driven, and treasured by few.

This quiet life was all that she knew.

She's not alone in this private zone.

 So many others, wives, sisters and many

misters share this oddest of druthers.

People will say and do anything in the presence of these folk.
They know your pin codes and
where the bodies are buried and best believe to their grave,
 your secrets will be carried.

Invisible people make the world go around.
You see them every day, but you'll never know their sound.

If no one cooked or did the wash,
 if no on taught, would your children learn?
 If no one cleaned houses,
drove the busses, tended to the sick, or made you look slick,
 then you would miss her.
You would surely miss these humanity gems.
These "hers" and these "hims".

Invisible people make the world go around.

About Daddy's Girl

There are many things that come to mind when considering the measure of a man. This next poem is inspired by fatherly love. Father, stepdad, grandfather. Call it what you will, but there is something to be said for the exceptional quality that turns the biggest men into the most wonderful, loving, supportive versions of themselves.

To all the dads that raise the bar,

Thank you.

DADDY'S GIRL

Too tiny to matter

And no one seems to care.

The world is so big and

So much seems unfair.

He makes it his quest

To right every wrong.

He tells the best stories

And hums made up songs.

The bar was set so high

He holds me when I cry.

There's nothing I can't do

In this world.

I'm a daddy's girl.

About Sisters

We had the honor of hosting a girl's night turkey dinner back in 2008. This poem was written, as a give-away for our friends that attended.

While preparing this book we are reminded of many of our loved ones that have struggled with an illness of one sort or

another. We are reminded to never hold back a kindness, to be present, to be kind and to be authentic.

We would like to take a brief pause to say thank you to our hard working, compassionate "Sisters" and "brothers" in healthcare.

Thank you very much for all that you do to make a positive difference in the lives of those who's lives that you touch,

Peachy Books Inc

SISTERS

Because the prettiest flowers come after the vine and the thorns.

Because the prettiest sunshine comes after the storm.

Because after the caterpillar worm, the butterfly appears.

That's you my dear.

And yet dearer and dearer our sisters become.

Because we are all

like grapes

on the vine,

getting

sweeter

with time

I love the misters too,

but I adore,

I adore,

 I adore and admire, my sisters like you.

About Complete

We live in a world surrounded by many amazing examples of enduring love.

See the elderly couple holding hands and walking along and one slows down instinctively knowing the other is a little worn from the journey.

We see him reach for her and her in turn and often the other has fallen asleep and we think it strange the quirky behavior of this lone person.

No, not quirky, just missing half of themselves. Can we be of assistance to such a person?

We, the human family, living in any place, at any time are in some measure, indebted to the silver hair that paved the way for us.

COMPLETE

He dares chance the unique of a delicious sunset. How does one set lest she rise?

He tastes deep sweet breathes that hint of summer's jasmine and ocean's breeze. She to breathes.

He is wooed as by her lovely voice and baby's coo and music flute and night owl and crickets to. Ear is seduced, she sings.

He fasts that palate not be altered, and reality thrown in squander when in that final moment he first finds his own.

He embraces tender touch on fingertip and cheek and lip and calloused hand as years pass by pretty crow's feet-slowly arrive.
Dark becomes grey and that to falls away.

He feels no dismay.

He is complete. She is the complement

ABOUT BEAUTY

The real beauty of humanity is just how similar we are.

We form groups and subgroups.

We move and speak differently.

We may live in completely different climate. But really, are we so different? On a global scale, we have more in common than not. Respect for our elders, family recipes and traditions. Humanity is so beautiful.

"BEAUTY IS AS BEAUTY DOES."

"Beauty is as Beauty does"

From perfect 10's to lucky 7's I'm all numbered out.

I'm not alone in this number zone of this there is no doubt.

Am I the ten that's dearly loved sent from above with head-turning
physique, a killer smile and a heart that's made of gold?
Brainy and bold, warm when life's cold?
Let's not forget stellar credit with good work ethic, soft hands &
tender voice am I sure to be the choice? Or am I more
like the two like you know who,
that seldom gets a dance, that rarely gets a chance, that scarcely gets a
glance?

I've a great sense of humor or so it's rumored and the jokes
that I tell are clean, they say laughter's a cure

so, you'll feel good for sure.
The silent smiles and decadent chews produced,

when to cook I'm induced with a grin.

"Encore, Encore" resounds through the place as all happily feed face.

Like a diamond in
the rough, a little scuffed up waiting for polish and shine
to show in time the meaning of refined.
I thinks that's who I am.

A ten or a two that's up to you. But as for me when a friend I see, I see
them as ten's not twos.
Good folks are good folks and I love em' just the same cause to me
we're all family.

It's been said that beauty is only skin deep. It takes time to learn the
truth in this quote.
Far too often we regret not considering this little life-saving note.
Beauty is as beauty does.
Humble heart, honest
tongue and noble mind.
These are but a few qualities in a life partner

the wise seek to find. So how will you choose? Either a friend,
confidant or mate?

Please do the double take and not choose by the outer alone. Misery
and eternal regrets are what many get when they forget that famous
age old quote,

"Beauty is as beauty does."

10's & 2's!

About Keep Swimming Upstream

This next poem is very personal to us. It has been well received by many friends and family members dealing with difficult trials. We hope that you enjoy it.

There are some trials that don't fall in the category of 'let it go'. They may be the sort of things that require action like complying with the medical care of a trusted and competent physician.

For the trials that we can choose to let go of, this next poem was written as a reminder to never give up, to continue to be the positive 'kind' of person.

KEEP SWIMMING UPSTREAM

No matter how tough the climb seems,

Keep swimming upstream. When the battle

seems lost and you can't afford the cost, Keep swimming upstream.

When negative words and spite like a bullet bite, Keep swimming
upstream.

When you've given your best to put strife to rest, Keep swimming
upstream.

Because the war is won one battle at a time, Keep swimming
upstream.

Because you were taught to be better regardless of the trials,
Keep swimming upstream.

So, when the going gets tough and you're about to give up, remember
that:
fish have scales and gills, birds have wings to fly and reach the highest
hills.

These are not talents but instinct, so how much more equipped are
you?

You that can think and decide
not to blink, twitch or stutter.

You that can think and no words or correct words and response utter?

Ah, so you see you are equipped. Don't trip, over your own fins, to the
other's chagrin.
Keep swimming upstream.

I mean think about the grace and ease
Of a school of fish in flight, how we delight, as we are pleased
But take note of what you don't see,
Not multi species, but they swim with their own and act according to
their 'kind'.

They only intermingle when on the hunt for the food they find. So,
what shall it be?

Will you be devoured by your foe?

By shrinking below and acting out of sorts?
This is a losing sport.

Keep swimming as you were trained, maintain,
stay the course.

Swim with best and away from the ways of the rest.

Keep swimming upstream!
Reach your dreams.

ABOUT A SIMPLE GIRL

I was grateful that I was able to share this with my Louisiana born and raised mother a few years before she fell asleep in death.

As I read it to her, I couldn't help but notice and I dearly appreciated noticing that it moved her to tears of appreciation.

She said she felt as if I were writing it from her perspective. The ability to reach a person on that level is an honor beyond description.

The fact that this was someone that I did and do love so dearly magnified the reward all the more.

I am humbled at the fact that others can journey and relate to the word pictures I am unworthy but grateful to paint.

A SIMPLE GIRL

I like crashing waves at the beach, Soul food,

home- made,
And oldies till dawn.
I make mistakes and ask lots of questions.

Am I easy to please?

I love to see happy children and people at peace. I

look forward to the day when all wars will cease.

Nothing warms my heart like a big bear hug.
It brought tears to my eyes when I saw a wife, father, mother, aunt,
grandmother, two sons and a daughter bring Juan's lunch to work the
other day.

I couldn't help but escape to nostalgic daydreams.

Back when I was little girl and mama would drive us cross country to
Aunt Josephine's house for: crab cakes, gumbo, collard greens and
Mardi Gras.
I never thought I'd miss Louisiana.

New Orleans showed us it's community, outhouses, southern accents,
pumping water from a well.

Lazy summer afternoons spent playing in the creek and flying bugs so
big we called them monsters.

New Orleans also showed us family feasts fit for a king, a deep-freezer
full of assorted beverages,

love and support with the biggest smiles

and the warmest hugs.

I hated being in the car with elbow to elbow people.

"Stop touching me! Mama! She's staring at me!"

"I want to sit in the front, it's my turn"
As we passed the time on the ride home with

"That's my car!"
"Wrong, you get that ugly one we just passed."

Only to be quieted by sleep, as mama looked in the back seat to discover

the entangled pretzel- like body of six children fast asleep.

ABOUT TIME IS MONEY

Time, a most priceless asset of the ages.

The great equalizer of the rich,

poor,

brilliant,

gifted

and average.

All men succumb to this master.

TIME IS MONEY

A wise woman once said that

"Time is Money",

when you ponder this, it may seem funny.

Because does that mean that the time we waste running around from chase to chase in meaningless pursuit of mundane endeavors is actually money spent?

Cash thrown away that should have been saved for a rainy day.

Now pay attention yawl

because I'm about to get deep.

I mean if time is money should we ever sleep?

And does this totally redefine the word cheap?

How much do you make spend or save in one day?

We all have 24 hours to pay, 60 seconds to save, 7 days to earn.

7 days to earn or 7 days to spend?
I mean if time were money you could guarantee tomorrow by how we spend right now.

How well we know,

that many times the actions of one moment have changed some people's lives forever.

Forever for better or forever for worse.

In that split second, did they purchase a curse?
Did they pay their way to an early grave?
Ah! Then time is money.

So, there's truth in this saying?
Now answer me this, for what are you paying?

Fame and fortune don't mean contentment.
You see they are more often linked with plain old' resentment.
The Eight or Nine decades we get

are far more valuable than any money spent

Ah then time is money,

and since time goes on forever,
plan wisely for your endeavors.

Let negativity ago, release it!
That's money thrown in the streets.

Be focused and genuine let your light shine.
Your descendants will praise you.

For a true legacy is not measured in dollars and cents.
If you hear what I tell you this time has been well spent.

Time is money yawl.

Times is Money,

But Money

Can

Not

buy Time!

ABOUT YOU GO GIRL

How beautiful the bond that doesn't suffer because one may have a moment of joy but rejoices in the shine as only a loyal and unselfish friend would.

Words come to mind like loyalty, sisterhood, trust, hope and love.

The talent of friendship, can we call it "friending?" 'Friending' is a talent. To those of you that have the talent of being a friend, or of having at least one true and loyal friend we admonish you to never take it for granted and to consider yourself fortunate.

Simply put,

"friendship is as friendship does."

To all of you that never take a true friend for granted,

that nourish and build up and love unconditionally,

thank you for being a true friend.

~ ~ ~

YOU GO GIRL!

When life brings you drama that makes you cling to your mamma,
You Go Girl!

Sometimes you want to scream because it seems you'll never reach
your dreams,
You Go Girl!

Like when everybody said you'd never make it halfway and their
negativity made you want to go crazy,
You Go Girl!

For not giving up but taking it like a champ when life gets you on the
chin,
You Go Girl!

In a world so filled with back-biting, doubt and stress, your
individuality, I must say, it does refresh one

so, you ...go ...

girl!

For remaining single and doing it well!
You Go Girl!

For being a true friend,
For marching at your own pace,
For the mother in you, the sister, the aunt,

the grandmother my ace,
For not changing a trace!
You Go Girl!

About She's So Lost

There are so many amazing young women with potential that goes unrealized. Talented artists, writers, painters, musicians, architects and so much more that goes undiscovered .

Could we help one of these young women to get back on their path? Invest the time to assure them that they are cared for and worth the effort?

SHE'S SO LOST

She's so lost.
She's mad and sad but outsiders observe and judge bad,
but she's lost.

Who will help her?
Guide her to the cure?
Help her stop sinking?
That not just a hottie with a body, but first young woman to comport
with dignity and gain respect?

To use the mind and perceive life's realities, that she's lost and on the
brink. What did you think when your helper came and helped you to
regain your way
to see clearly that you were nearly?

at failure's door?

Failure to find who and what you could really be. Reaching life's
potential of a productive life.

Oh, it's fast, fun and flippant at first. But make no mistake, for we all
have Adam's curse of growing old and eventually dying.

She's lost and not even trying.
So not slowly dying but rushing
to bring hurt and hurting and crying and

rapidly, dying.

No quality of life,
no mentality of a wife or a productive life. But strife.

Strife that comes when reality hits too late and unfulfilled hopes
or baby daddy times three becomes reality.

She's so lost. There's a mister where there should be a mom, dad
or big sister.

She's been taught that she ought to-'use what she's got'
To dress for the spot-light of men with minds not right.

'That the flesh and appearance are her best life
defense?'

She's so lost.
A brother can love and try but it takes an involved parent or
a big sister to guide

through body changes uncertainty, emotional
fragility, angry and unsure confused and lashing out physically,
verbally... all the while really saying... HELP ME!

She's drowning...

Slowly.

She's just lost,

Guide the little girls home,

before they pay a disastrous cost!

ABOUT SIMPLE THINGS

Because we are delighted to include a poem about cherished keepsakes like a favorite coffee mug or scarf or mules that we hope never wear out because we have travelled so many miles wearing them and even perhaps written about them. Journaling comes to mind when we read poems like this. What a peachy way to treasure our fondest memories. What's more enjoyable that keeping a personal record of the small moments that were the building blocks of our lives.

SIMPLE THINGS

Flakes of snow that glisten in the night.

Small grains of rice that keep families fed.

Gentle drops of water that become water falls.

Simple things that we delight to recall.

Crisp laundered sheets that feel best after a bath.

Rose petals that become treasured keepsakes.

The sound of children laughing as they run down the hall.

Simple things that we delight to recall.

Tiny hands that grow up to save the day.

Tender embrace after a long time away.

The best candle aroma that we enjoy most of all.

Simple things that we delight to recall.

A single musical note that gives birth to a song.

A quick kiss farewell that makes your heart melt.

The last flicker of candle wick before we say, "good night" to all.

Simple things that we delight to recall.

About If We Treated

This next poem is inspired by simpler times. Times when most people knew and could trust their neighbors. Simpler times and when families sat and ate meals together or not at all.

Even if we take a brief moment out of our busy lives to be kind to today's youth, we and they will be better for it.

IF WE TREATED

If we treated people, the way we treat our cars,

Our ancestors would be the real super stars.

A lifetime of teaching that our hearts they'd be reaching. Never sparing the rod to save sons. Do we smile when we see these rare ones and ask where they came from?

If we treated people, the way we treat cars. We'd polish them up to show them off, when they grow old and rare.
Like aging frail grandparents with beautiful white hair.

We wouldn't pass by without taking long notice.
But would write what they taught so later we could quote it.

We would take pictures with them and tell tales of their travels.
Even when they've grown old and seem to slowly unravel.

If we treated people, the way we treat our cars. We would keep good records of their every need.

Like oil changes, tune ups, and tire rotations. We'd make notations of their many quotations.

Hanging on to every word, looking at them with pride. Knowing that we came from inside, their heart and inner parts.

This is our trust.
To do what we must to return the love that was shown to us.

What did we teach?

Wait till they're buying, waxing and buffing their own.

All grown up with priorities and stuff.

Will it be rough?

To see ourselves in them?

Will they cherish as we taught?

Or will their concern be for the thing they bought?

Waxed and shined up with chrome rims and woofers.

This, 'four wheeled big deal.'

If we get where we're going without ever slowing,

to care, to thank, to express the gratitude we feel.
The young ones are watching and need to be shown the way.

Be quick to pause and show.

A moment to invest in the future of our youth.

Teaching them the truth.

Our treasure is aging.

Our treasure will soon be sleeping.

Their memory we'll be keeping.

The true classics we have.

If we treat people, the way we treat cars.

ABOUT IF A TREE FALLS

If a Tree Falls was inspired by a beautiful

forest that was observed with a random fallen tree. The tree was surrounded by a gorgeous mountain backdrop. As it lay there nestled among its healthy standing friends, it appeared to be just

pausing for an enviable siesta.

We benefit so much from sustainable

forestry. Clean drinking water, habitats,

for endangered species, home building

supplies, furniture, paper, pencils,

cotton and so much more.

Most people are surprised to find out that

forestry generates a sizeable revenue that

is comparable to the automotive industry.

Many communities owe their financial

solvency to that four-letter word,

t-r-e-e.

IF A TREE FALLS

If a tree falls In the forest will it make a little sound?

That's the last thing that we think when we see it laying down.

All that money on the ground...

If a tree falls In the forest

Will we once again be blessed?

If a tree falls In the forest

Will anybody hear it

Come near it?

If a tree falls In the forest

Will anyone claim it?

Name it?

Say they saw it, that they called it?

That it belongs them alone?

If a tree falls In the forest

Will there be jobs for all of the men folk?

And will my friends move back again?

If a tree falls In the forest

Will momma yell surprise

and we get new school supplies?

If a tree falls In the forest

Will our schoolbooks be brand new?

Instead of all marked up and used?

Scented with years past fumes.

A little sticky at times with inserted rhymes.

If a tree falls In the forest

Will winter be less cold?

And we have wood for the stove?

If a tree falls In the forest

and it's just after the rain,

will we feel blessed again?

ABOUT THOUSANDAIRE MAN

This next poem was written with that creative, self-starter in mind. A person willing to risk

public opinion to be their own person.

Some poems are written to make you laugh and some to make you think. Here's one

written to do a little of both.

Enjoy this light-hearted poem as you share this next "Candle" with us.

THOUSANDAIRE MAN

What kind of a man can pick up the tab when you're on date without looking drab?

A Thousandaire man can.

What sort of a man can mix bold prints and create new fashionable trends?

Trends like wearing strange sox in a drop top Benz.

A Thousandaire man can.

What man dare make it so,

unlike many men we know,

have a stock portfolio with more than two zeros?

A Thousandaire man can.

See anybody can inherit a house or even a million,

Have a viral video with likes by the zillions

Online followers in the cajillions...

But people stop and stare

at the self -made man over there.

That resourceful sort,

such a clever sport,

so dapper and debonair,

Just look at him...

that handsome, .

that man,

that …

Thousandaire.

About Doing Too Much

This is what some people call the mantra of our decade. We all have different energy levels, interests and talents.

No one should feel the need to gage their personal worth solely based on how they compare to the talents or limitations of another. "Don't compare your beginning to someone else's ending" is the thought that comes to mind.

It feels good to compliment the difference and successful accomplishments of others.

In order to develop your gift, you have to find it and that's a lot harder to do when we are focusing on someone else's personal score card.

Doing Too Much

I be doing too much

My minds in a rush

Some say chill and hush

But this vibe I can't crush.

Cause the vibe that I stop

Could be the first drop

As the message starts to flow

And creatively I grow

So here I go

Here I go…

Doing Too much.

About Two Brown Girls

Because childhood memories of time with our friends are priceless. We were literally made of energy and the activities of the day lent themselves to friends being metronomes of a sort.

From songs that we sang to the tandem bikes that we rode, friendship meant working as a team to create fun moments outdoors without television and electronic gadgets.

TWO BROWN GIRLS

Two brown girls were playing in the park.

Double Dutch singing till just before dark.

Two brown girls, mastering jump rope and jacks.

Having so much fun, they turned the clock hands back.

Two brown girls as time whisked by.

Brave enough to dare, slightly afraid to try.

Two brown girls fishing in favorite pond.

Two brown Girls facing fears and forging bonds.

Two brown girls surpassing life's tests.

Trials overcome, against all odds, while over the shoulder,
they look back to give and receive a reassuring nod.

Two brown girls.

Imparting confidence.

"You've got this".

There's no trial or test,

No too heavy a whirl,

That we can't face and surpass.

Two brown girls.

About Hairstyle?

Why not? Women have to juggle so many things.

We are writers, daughters, teachers, mothers, employees,

business owners, athletes,

caregivers, trendsetters and so much more. In this

modern era of expression and acceptance, women have

the license to do more than ever before.

Ladies, here is your permission to be fabulous, but listen

to your friends.

HAIRSTYLE

So, it's my hair the last time I checked

if I wear it up or way down my neck.

I might wear it blond

or slicked -back - black.

I might get the itch for a side pony tail.

Whatever I choose my hair never fails.

Like the curly fro

when I'm on the go.

Maybe corn rows

one by one…

when I'm in the mood for a little hair fun.

When I'm dolled up for the sun

and I wear a cute fancy bun

the look on your face surely makes me want to run.

Cause I'm tired of explaining

about my fabulous interchanging

Hairstyles

Some smile

at my free styles

like a short wig

can you dig?

If you don't like it…

then don't look.

Cause you're not debating

it's simply hating.

When you see me

its jealousy

that stops your smile

and talk wild

all the while …

about my…

Hairstyle.

Or at least that's what I tell myself.

Maybe I should have paid heed

When you gave the advice that I surely did need.

Hairstyle?

ABOUT GOLDEN SUNRAYS

It has been observed that people are often so busy that they are almost on autopilot. If you ask around, you might be surprised by how many people go from day to without being able to recall highlights of important conversations.

A beautiful moment that actually sank in without the desire to see it behind a lens or even post about it. The memories that we capture are great to share later. Sometimes though, that insatiable desire to selfie everything, can spoil a beautiful little innocent moment that was only meant to be enjoyed in the here and now.

Another by-product of our busy mindset is the procrastination that results from a failure to make confident decisions.

As you complete your many necessary to-do items, we ask that you regularly pause for a bit of guilt free "me time".

Here is a "Candle" to help you to relax.

GOLDEN SUNRAYS

Golden sunrays floating, to and fro every day.

Persistent golden waves, the power they display.

Golden sunrays, so beautiful, radiant and
strong.

Ocean's might, the unending source of song.

Golden sunrays that tempt toes and little feet.

Nourishing sunrays, gently drifting past my face.

Ocean's waves, we need a happy place.

LITTLE MISS AND THE MOUNTAIN

Because sometimes we all need the power of an active imagination. The power to focus on what we can do instead of dreadfully dwelling on the obstacles that may hinder us from reaching our goals. Little Miss and the Mountain shows how we can push ahead no matter how formidable the mountains of today and climb them all one step at a time.

LITTLE MISS AND THE MOUNTAIN

There once stood a girl.

She was a so small,

to small, not tall enough at all girl.

Her tresses were a mess, worn shoes and tattered dress. She lived by
the sea side and happened to reside…

Near the meanest mountain full of mean trees.

She was afraid of the mountain and afraid of its bees.

That the mountain was mean, and no one dared dispute.

But our little girl was ever so bold and equally cute.

She started the day with a hop from her bed. Straight to the mountain,
she surely would head.

Loud waves would crash as they came to and fro.

But once our girl started shouting, the wave's tone seemed low.

"We need what grows freely at your side. So, I'm coming up mountain, I've got the sea on my side! So, give me what I need, or I promise you this, if you're mean to me, you'll face the sea's mist.

Convinced was our girl that the mountain did hear, she went up the mountain with no trace of fear.

This girl so small, too small

not tall at all enough for the world girl.

As it turns out was not so very small at all.

ABOUT A MOST UNLIKELY FRIENDSHIP

This next short book is an abbreviated version of "A Most Unlikely Friendship" There is a purity and beauty that is often found in our younger selves. This is a fictional account about the unselfish nature of a friendship between a baby flamingo and a baby bald eagle.

This book was inspired by the love we all have in our hearts for children around the world that for one reason or another have ever been hospitalized.

A Most Unlikely Friendship:

I was a lone little egg, aware of nothing outside my shell.

Nested safely beneath parent's warmth I was doing just swell. Safely I grew and only mother knew, she would sway as she counted the days.

"One day soon,

my young one,

you'll come out and feel warm sun."

She would sing her promise song and to see her I did long. She sang of beautiful beaches and delicious treats.

One day her song was interrupted and replaced by such a sound. There was loud noise and squawking heard all around. I quivered in my egg and suddenly began to fall. I only remember my mother's gentle cry and falling, falling, falling so far and so very fast.

My fall was halted by the kind, big, black bird that carried me to her home. "Safety at last," I naïvely thought. Now I was at 'peace' to reflect and dissect and make sense of all that had just occurred.

This tranquil would not last long. Suddenly came the sound,

"Run little bird, run little one, run this way fast!"

She was but a tiny version of the one that 'saved' me.

Why would I leave my place of safety?

Alas instinct was speaking and with little to no reason,

I saw it wise to follow my little guide. I fled from once thought safe place and followed new friend.

"Stay here new friend till I return again, or sadly my mother will be you end".

Neath nearby ledge, I kept quiet till night, as new friend told me, I sat shivering, cold and out of sight. New friend's mother did quickly return. But I hid safely out of sight, new friend gave me food and a secret place to reside.

Friend's mother was desperate, as she looked for her find, she squeaked and she squawked and cried out to find, her frightened dinner guest that tried desperately to hide.

Nights became days and I happily did amaze to see new friend arrive. Promise was kept and soon I could see, friend kept her word and came back for me.

"Follow my steps and do not look back! For quickly we must go, heed my every track."

"Why is this happening?", I thought in way backs of my mind. I am grateful for new friend; she most certainly is the life- saving kind. Weeks became months and months became years; we did grow as friends to shed life's many fears.

We passed the time with joy sublime. We swam in warm waters, travelled valleys and cliffs. All of these joys I did share because a dear friend showed care. "How can I repay her, this loyal friend of mine?" I often did think. Why be so kind to me? I'm so little, so pink. A loyal dear one to share all of life's fun. We like the same things. She soars while I sing.

We laugh at night winds that tickle our wings. Not long did I wait, for a chance to repay her. For friend soon faced certain peril. Hunter was strong, with teeth so long and a might to fight to make friend his meal. Friend fought as she could, and I quickly rushed to the sound of her call. Dear friend was soon to meet life's demise. I suddenly appeared to hunter's startled eyes. Bravely I fought to hunter's surprise!

I kicked and I squawked, I yelled, bit and shouted.

Legs over wings

over teeth

over things!

I fought with all that I had, and I held nothing back, it was my turn to save, for my friend I'd be brave. Brief relief was realized as I soon surmised, that dear friend was free from life ending jaws. Dear friend ran free but soon stopped to return and ensure safety for me. Hunter was beat by two and not one. For this true friendship was not ready to yet be un-done. We patched up our wounds and wept in relief, that hunter was not today a victorious thief.

I did happily repay my friend in this way and wouldn't you know, we are friends to this day.

Alas,

I have told you so many details of this

exciting little story.

I have yet to reveal the names of dear friend and me.

I am Phoebe the flamingo and dear friend,

is Loyola the beautiful loyal balled eagle.

Friendship is as friendship does, choose your friends patiently and wisely. Beauty is as beauty does. True, loyal, enduring friendship is beautiful, rare and worth the wait.

When last they were seen, these little friends were holding hands and dancing off into the sunset.

This story was written for every child that forms an unlikely friendship and

manages to unselfishly put those interest ahead of their own regardless of personal loss or sacrifice.

 (There were a lot of lessons in this friendship story. How many did you notice? Please tell us on Instagram at peachybooks4u or email us at meetblue@mail.com)

About introduction to the "Meet Blue" series

As an added treat, for those of you with small children in your lives, we want to share something with you from our upcoming "Meet Blue" series.

MEET BLUE-BLUE'S FIRST FLIGHT

Let's Learn Our Colors

From his very first flight, Blue found a delight.

To be up in the sky and see the sky sights.

Blue saw birds and planes.

Blue flew on top of the rain.

Blue smiled at rainbow colors and soon would know the name of each one.

There was so much to be see and so much to be done. This was the very first day Blue flew up near the sun.

Blue flew past a plane and decided to glide, when he saw his friends sitting safely inside.

Some were fast asleep and others mussing about. Blue was ever so excited but would not shout.

Blue flew down below and what do you know, he saw more of his friends, sitting neatly in rows.

Friends were sitting in class and coloring that day. They were coloring the fun -rainbow way.

They learned to spell and to call them all by name. They even played a coloring game.

They colored with orange, with red and with blue. They colored neatly in the lines as they were taught to do.

When teacher quizzed students to name the color of a thing
,
they answered correctly before the school bell did ring.

The End

BLUE MEETS LITTLE SHOE

Little Shoe, Little Shoe, how do you do?

Little Shoe, Little Shoe my name is Blue.

Little Shoe, Little Shoe it's nice to meet you.

Little Shoe, Little Shoe let's eat fruit.

Little Shoe, Little Shoe neatly on feet.

Little Shoe, Little Shoe never on the seat.

Little Shoe, Little Shoe neatly placed away.

Little Shoe, Little Shoe now let's play.

Little Shoe and Blue

Little Shoe and Blue

I'm glad to meet you.

The End

About The Fluffiest Bed in Town

One of the modern additions to many homes is a charging station. A place where cell phones and computer gadgets are kept

dry and plugged in to charge up and refresh.

Children have an equivalent of a charging station. It's called a bed. This next story is our way of wishing you sweet dreams as you and your little readers tuck into bed and refresh for either a nap time of a night of blissful rest.

The Fluffiest Bed in Town

The fluffiest bed in town was softer than the softest down.

The fluffiest bed in town was in a room with cookies brown.

The fluffiest bed in town was sure to heal a frown and would block out any sound.

The fluffiest bed in town was as fluffy as the puffiest cloud and as soft as it could be.

The fluffiest bed in town was such a joy to see and just big enough for me.

The fluffiest bed in town was soft to tiny toes. Soft to little nose and soft to tiny elbows.

The fluffiest bed in town was the very best place to end the very best day.

With a deep breath in and a gentle whisper out we take turns to say, at the end of each day...

"Good night nose, good night toes,
good night to tiny elbows."

"Good night dear family, kind and
true,

and please remember

I love you.

Sweet fluffy dreams."

The End

Thank you for enjoying

a few "Candles" with us.

Please check out other books by Peachy Books Inc. current and upcoming titles:

Meet Blue (Series)-The Day that Orange Met Blue

- The Day that Happy Met Blue

- Blue Meets Nap Time

-Blue's First Flight, Let's Learn our Colors (fully illustrated)

-Blue Meets Little Shoe (fully illustrated)

The Queen of too Much Stuff

A Most Unlikely Friendship (fully Illustrated)

Little Miss and the Mountain (fully illustrated)

The Fluffiest Bed in Town (fully illustrated)

Duke and Dirk (Series)-Health Helpers (A patient inspired children's activity book)   -Duke and Dirk Meet Recycle Rob

-Duke and Dirk's First Day of School

Guess What (Series) All of Our Cars Have Names (A four-part series)
-Guess What? This is my big sister book

- Guess What? Nobody is **GOODER** than Anyone Else

- Guess What? We can greet in over ten languages
- Guess What? This is my big brother book
- Guess What? This is how we wash our hands
-Guess What? This is how we fly on an airplane

Peachybooks@mail.com

Peachybooks.org

Instagram-Peachybooks4u

©□ 2020 Peachy Books Inc.

ISBN 9798603566610